THE
CineTarot
DECK & SYSTEM

GO TO THE MOVIES & MASTER THE TAROT

WRITTEN & DESIGNED BY
Devin KORDT-THOMAS

INTUITIVE KEY

This edition first published in 2021 by Intuitive Key Consulting LLC

Copyright 2021 Devin Kordt-Thomas
All rights reserved. No part of this publication may be reproduced, stored or transmitted in any form or by any means, electronic, mechanical, photocopying, recording, scanning, or otherwise without written permission from the publisher. It is illegal to copy this book, post it to a website, or distribute it by any other means without permission.

Neither author or publisher have any responsibility for the persistence or accuracy of URLs for external or third-party Internet Websites referred to in this publication and does not guarantee that any content on such Websites is, or will remain, accurate or appropriate.

Designations used by companies to distinguish their products are often claimed as trademarks. All brand names and product names used in this book and on its cover are trade names, service marks, trademarks and registered trademarks of their respective owners. The publishers and the book are not associated with any product or vendor mentioned in this book. None of the companies referred to within the book have endorsed the book.

The illustrations, cover design, diagrams, and contents are fully protected by copyright. No part of this book may be reproduced in any form without permission in writing from the publisher, except by a reviewer who wishes to quote brief passages in connection with a review written for inclusion in a magazine, newspaper, or website.

ISBNs: Print: 978-1-7369695-5-7 (hardcover)
       Print: 978-1-7369695-2-6 (trade paperback)
       EPUB: 978-1-7369695-4-0
       Kindle: 978-1-7369695-7-1
       PDF: 978-1-7369695-8-8

Library of Congress Cataloguing-in-Publication Data available upon request.

www.intuitivekey.com & www.cinetarot.com

DEDICATION

With gratitude to my teachers and spiritual companions of the three times, to all lovers of cinema, and to you and your innate psychic potential and abilities.

PREFACE

As a consultant psychic medium, intuition coach, and certified psychic development teacher, I often use the tarot and its symbolism as a jumping-off point for divination. Over the years I have seen many novice tarot card readers struggle to master the meanings of the cards. The esoteric symbolism found in traditional decks is not always easily remembered, and can be unnecessarily challenging. What successful tarot readers discover is that you must reconcile your understanding of the tarot symbols with your own personal symbolic language. They must be relevant to you.

As an avid filmgoer and actor, I have always enjoyed film's ability to transport you to other times and other worlds, or allow you to experience the highs and lows of the human condition through a compelling story. In using the tarot, I discovered that the information I received from the cards often unfolded like scenes in a movie, and that the figures aligned with certain actors and the famous characters they embodied.

With the CineTarot deck and system, I have created a contemporary way to read the tarot that offers both novice and master readers a means to swiftly tap into their innate intuition. Each tarot card is interpreted in the context of a specific movie, central character, theme, and genre, drawing on a selection of films that range from famous classics to buried treasures. For the 22 Major Arcana (secrets or mysteries) cards, traditional card names are juxtaposed with key movie characters; in the case of the 14 Minor Arcana court cards, I have assigned each a corresponding iconic actor based on their body of work and screen persona. Esoteric keys (elements, planets, astrological correspondence, and Hebrew Kabbalah references) are also included for more advanced readers.

The visual design of each card is inspired by minimalistic movie poster art, and employs key geometric shapes and an evocative color palette to convey the overall theme of each film. Each card's divinatory logline is infused with keywords that capture the essence of the film while still expressing the classical meaning of the card.

As the reading progresses, think of each card as a "scene" in a film that is speaking uniquely to you. Whether you're reading for yourself or others, you'll be amazed at how easy it is to communicate the meaning of the tarot through the universal language of film.

Let's go to the movies—and master the tarot!

CONTENTS

Preface	VII
The Major Arcana	11
0: The Fool	14
I: The Magician	16
II: The High Priestess	18
III: The Empress	20
IV: The Emperor	22
V: The High Priest	24
VI: The Lovers	26
VII: The Chariot	28
VIII: Justice	30
IX: The Hermit	32
X: Wheel of Fortune	34
XI: Strength	36
XII: The Hanged Man	38
XIII: Death	40
XIV: Temperance	42
XV: The Devil	44
XVI: The Tower	46
XVII: The Star	48
XVIII: The Moon	50
XIX: The Sun	52
XX: Judgement	54
XXI: The World	56
The Minor Arcana Court Cards	59
King of Wands	64
Queen of Wands	66
Knight of Wands	68
Page of Wands	70
King of Cups	72
Queen of Cups	74
Knight of Cups	76
Page of Cups	78
King of Swords	80
Queen of Swords	82
Knight of Swords	84
Page of Swords	86
King of Coins	88

Queen of Coins	90
Knight of Coins	92
Page of Coins	94
The CineTarot Reading	97
The Trailer	100
The Three Acts Reading	101
The Feature	102
About The Author	107

THE MAJOR ARCANA

THE MAJOR ARCANA

The first 22 cards of the CineTarot deck are the Major Arcana (secrets or mysteries), the most familiar and impactful cards in a tarot deck. While the Minor Arcana cards focus on the everyday actions and decisions you must face, the Major Arcana cards reveal messages about the bigger picture of your life and its long-term direction, and each offers a specific message of perspective and guidance to help you in times of need.

Taken together, the Major Arcana represent the soul's conscious, subconscious, and superconscious drives, and contain one's karmic goals, past lives, current situation, and future activities. They constitute a grand narrative of the accomplishments, setbacks, and lessons we all learn as we go through the trials and tribulations of our lives, growing into whole, complete beings by the end of our journey. Many tarot card readers find that these 22 cards are all they need to provide an accurate reading.

Though each of the Major Arcana cards stands alone, with its own distinctive meanings and influences, together they tell a story. The first card, the Fool (card number 0), is the main character of this story, and the 21 cards that follow represent the steps on his journey through life toward the ultimate goal of self-realization, each card illustrating a key life lesson and a milestone to be achieved in this personal odyssey.

As the Fool embarks on his path, he navigates both the material and the spiritual world with a sense of openness and a yearning for adventure. Along the way, he encounters mentors who coach him on how to complete each life lesson, and advise him on how to best navigate the tests and adversities ahead. The Fool always has the option to reject the lesson or refuse to move forward to achieve the goal—but moving forward offers rewards, while refusing the lesson results in frustration and stagnation.

0
THE FOOL

"My! People come and go so quickly here!"
—Dorothy Gale

The Fool as Dorothy
Film: *The Wizard of Oz* (1939)
Genre: Adventure

Divinatory Logline:
An innocent young girl and her dog embark on an adventure of self-discovery and personal growth when she is transported from the dualistic, black-and-white world of rural Kansas to a multi-faceted magical land over the rainbow filled with challenges, opportunities, and colorful characters that seem oddly familiar.

Inverted: Will her naïveté, folly, and inattention distract her from her true path?

Esoteric Keys
Element: △ Air
Planet: ♅ Uranus
Numerology: 0 (Zero)
Hebrew: א Alef Ox: Primordial Energy

THE MAJOR ARCANA

I
THE MAGICIAN

"It does not do well to dwell on dreams and forget to live."
—Albus Dumbledore

The Magician as Harry Potter
Film: *Harry Potter and the Sorcerer's Stone* (2001)
Genre: Adventure

Divinatory Logline:
An enthusiastic orphan discovers the truth about his birthright and his potential to become a powerful wizard. He begins his studies at boarding school to develop his capabilities through concentration and self-mastery in order to combat the negative forces that stand in his way.

Inverted: Can he overcome his hesitation and indecision in order to realize his skills and put them to good use, or will he apply his willpower to destructive ends—or waste it through lack of diligence?

Esoteric Keys
Element: ⌂ Air
Planet: ☿ Mercury
Numerology: I (One)
Hebrew: ב Bet House: Temple, Attraction

THE MAJOR ARCANA

II
THE HIGH PRIESTESS

"When God fights, it's of small consequence whether the hand that holds the sword is big or little."
—Jeanne d'Arc

The High Priestess as Jeanne d'Arc
Film: *La passion de Jeanne d'Arc* (1928)
Genre: Biography, Drama, History

Divinatory Logline:
In 1431 France, a selfless and pure peasant girl is called to God through a series of visions and is subsequently placed on trial for heresy by the male-dominated Church, whose judges forcefully attempt to have her recant her exalted state and awakening.

Inverted: Will her divine exuberance be tempered so that it is no longer threatening to the status quo, or will her spiritual spark lead to her demise?

Esoteric Keys
Element: ∇ Water
Planet: ☽ The Moon
Numerology: II (Two)
Hebrew: ג Gimel Camel: Lifting Up, Unconscious

THE MAJOR ARCANA

III
THE EMPRESS

"I am the Nile. I will have sons. Isis has told me ... My breasts are full of love and life. My hips are rounded and well apart. Such women, they say, have sons."
—Cleopatra

The Empress as Cleopatra
Film: *Cleopatra* **(1963)**
Genre: Biography, Drama, History

Divinatory Logline:
As a young ruler and fertile queen, Cleopatra of Egypt must navigate the safety of both her nation (against a military invasion by Rome) and her heart (against the entreaties of her two suitors, the Roman emperor Julius Caesar and his bold general Marc Antony) or perish in her attempt.

Inverted: Will her head or heart rule her decisions?

Esoteric Keys
Element: ▽ Earth
Planet: ♀ Venus
Numerology: III (Three)
Hebrew: ד Dalet Door: Pathway, Nourishment

THE MAJOR ARCANA

IV
THE EMPEROR

"I'm gonna make him an offer he can't refuse."
—Don Corleone

The Emperor as Don Corleone
Film: *The Godfather* **(1972)**
Genre: Crime, Drama

Divinatory Logline:
The worldly patriarch of an Italian-American organized crime family, driven by intelligence and reason rather than emotion, sets the wheels in motion for a transfer of power to his youngest son in order to maintain his legacy.

Inverted: Will he have enough strength to maintain control and keep his arrogance, megalomania, and rashness in check?

Esoteric Keys
Element: △ Fire
Astrology: ♈ Aries (Active, Demanding, Determined, Effective, Ambitious)
Numerology: IV (Four)
Hebrew: ה He Window: Vision, Reasoning

THE MAJOR ARCANA

V
THE HIGH PRIEST

"I am a Muslim and a Hindu and a Christian and a Jew, and so are all of you."
—Gandhi

The High Priest as Gandhi
Film: *Gandhi* **(1982)**
Genre: Biography, Drama, History

Divinatory Logline:
British-educated lawyer Mohandas Gandhi returns to his native India and leverages both his legal skills and his spiritual strength and conviction as he works toward Indian independence from Britain, challenging an empire while living a life of austerity and service.

Inverted: Will he be able to place his trust in others to achieve his goals, or will his single-minded focus and stubbornness alienate those closest to him?

Esoteric Keys
Element: ▽ Earth
Astrology: ♉ Taurus (Grounded, Tough, Appreciative, Diligent, Patient)
Numerology: V (Five)
Hebrew: ו Vav Hook, Nail: Connections, Secure

THE MAJOR ARCANA

VI
THE LOVERS

"There's a place for us, a time and place for us,
Hold my hand and we're halfway there,
Hold my hand and I'll take you there,
Somehow, someday, somewhere!"
—Maria & Tony

The Lovers as Maria & Tony
Film: *West Side Story* **(1961)**
Genre: Crime, Drama, Musical

Divinatory Logline:
This musical reinterpretation of Romeo and Juliet set in the slums of the upper West Side of Manhattan pits the promise and power of a young couple's new love against their loyalty to their respective rival gangs and the friends whom they are also bound to.

Inverted: Can the lovers overcome the trials, prejudices, and turf wars or will they fail to meet the test, resulting in separation and their love perishing like a fragile flower in the asphalt jungle?

Esoteric Keys
Element: ▽ Earth
Astrology: ♊ Gemini (Communicative, Indecisive, Inquisitive, Intelligent, Changeable)
Numerology: VI (Six)
Hebrew: ז Zayin Sword: Discernment, Cut Off

THE MAJOR ARCANA

VII
THE CHARIOT

"Get your motor runnin',
Head out on the highway,
Lookin' for adventure,
And whatever comes our way"
—Steppenwolf, "Born to be Wild"

The Chariot as Wyatt (Captain America)
Film: *Easy Rider* (1969)
Genre: Adventure, Drama

Divinatory Logline:
Two biker buddies embark on a cross-country journey from Los Angeles to New Orleans, experience the gap between aspirational ideals and the forces of blind patriotism and small-town prejudice, and ultimately realize that their sense of freedom is illusory.

Inverted: Can peace be maintained on the highway of life, or will an empty gas tank result in a sudden collapse before the journey's end?

Esoteric Keys
Element: ▽ Water
Astrology: ♋ Cancer (Emotional, Diplomatic, Intense, Impulsive, Selective)
Numerology: VII (Seven)
Hebrew: ח Het Field, Fence: Separate, Enclose

THE MAJOR ARCANA

VIII
JUSTICE

"Well, I think testimony that can put a boy into the electric chair should be that accurate."
—Juror 8

Justice as Juror 8
Film: *12 Angry Men* (1957)
Genre: Crime, Drama

Divinatory Logline:
As a jury debates the fate of a Puerto Rican teenager accused of murdering his father, Juror 8 slows the jury's prejudicial rush toward a guilty verdict and likely death sentence to ensure impartiality and maintain the balance of justice.

Inverted: Can each juror's bias and personal interests be set aside in the service of justice, or will shoddy analysis, intolerance, and bias result in an unfair outcome?

Esoteric Keys
Element: △ Air
Astrology: ♎ Libra (Balanced, Fair, Honors Truth, Beauty, and Perfection)
Numerology: VIII (Eight)
Hebrew: ל Lamed Goad, Staff: Prod, Tongue

THE MAJOR ARCANA

IX
THE HERMIT

"Hell is empty and all the devils are here."
—Prospero

The Hermit as Prospero
Film: *Prospero's Books* **(1991)**
Genre: Drama, Fantasy

Divinatory Logline:
Prospero, the exiled duke of Milan and a possessor of secrets, emerges from his island-bound seclusion to use his alchemical skills for revenge by creating a tempest that shipwrecks his foes, and must then further bring his enemies under his control to thwart his daughter's ill-matched romance.

Inverted: Will Prospero's overprotectiveness, retrospection, and failure to face facts hinder his efforts toward concrete action, or will he be able to successfully re-emerge into the broader world?

Esoteric Keys
Element: ▽ Earth
Astrology: ♍ Virgo (Analyzing, Practical, Reflective, Observant, Thoughtful)
Numerology: IX (Nine)
Hebrew: י Yod Closed Hand: Deed, Work

X
WHEEL OF FORTUNE

"I'm sorry, Dave. I'm afraid I can't do that."
—HAL 9000

The Wheel of Fortune as HAL 9000
Film: *2001: A Space Odyssey* (1968)
Genre: Adventure, Sci-fi

Divinatory Logline:
Following the discovery of an otherworldly black structure beneath the moon's surface, the origin and destiny of mankind is explored across a time and space continuum when a team of astronauts embarks on an ill-fated secret mission aided (and then menaced) by an advanced supercomputer, HAL 9000.

Inverted: Will man's dependency on technology result in erratic and unpredictable results?

Esoteric Keys
Element: Δ Fire
Planet: ♃ Jupiter
Numerology: X (Ten) (1)
Hebrew: כ Kaf Open Hand: Cover, Grasp

THE MAJOR ARCANA

XI
STRENGTH

"You let a woman beat ya, huh?"
—Gloria

Strength as Gloria
Film: *Gloria* (1980)
Genre: Crime, Drama, Thriller

Divinatory Logline:
When gangsters kill a young boy's family, a Mafioso's former mistress comes to the child's aid as a reluctant but determined protectress, shielding him with her smarts and determination while exerting leverage over their pursuers with a book of accounting records the mob is desperate to obtain at any cost.

Inverted: Under what terms can the strong protect the weak without abusing power and falling victim to the peril that threatens them both?

Esoteric Keys
Element: △ Fire
Astrology: ♌ Leo (Ruling, Warm, Generous, Loyal, Motivated)
Numerology: XI (Eleven) (2)
Hebrew: ט Tet Serpent, Twist: Surround

THE MAJOR ARCANA

XII
THE HANGED MAN

"What can I do?"
—Lola

The Hanged Man as Lola
Film: *Run Lola Run* (1998)
Genre: Crime, Drama, Thriller

Divinatory Logline:
Lola's life is both suspended and accelerated when her desperate, race-against-the-clock attempt to salvage her gangster boyfriend's failed money drop leads her toward three very different fates.

Inverted: In the face of multiple options, will the self-centeredness of ego be overcome by an effort to move forward and escape stagnation, or will a loss of faith slow your pace and result in defeat?

Esoteric Keys
Element: ∇ Water
Planet: ♆ Neptune
Numerology: XII (Twelve) (3)
Hebrew: מ Mem Water: Overpower, Reversal

THE MAJOR ARCANA

XIII

DEATH

"Horror and moral terror are your friends.
If they are not, then they are enemies to be feared."
—Colonel Walter E. Kurtz

Death as Colonel Walter E. Kurtz
Film: *Apocalypse Now* **(1979)**
Genre: Drama, Mystery, War

Divinatory Logline:
Transformation and death are explored against the backdrop of the Vietnam war when US Army officer Captain Willard is tasked with tracking down and terminating Colonel Kurtz, a Green Beret who has gone rogue.

Inverted: Can Kurtz be brought back from the heart of darkness, or will his brilliant mind succumb to the horrors of war?

Esoteric Keys
Element: ▽ Water
Astrology: ♏ Scorpio: Transient, Self-Willed, Purposeful, Unyielding
Numerology: XIII (Thirteen) (4)
Hebrew: נ Nun Fruit, Fish: Sprouting, Activity, Life

THE MAJOR ARCANA

XIV
TEMPERANCE

"Life should be lived on the edge of life."
—Philippe

Temperance as Philippe Petit
Film: *Man on Wire* (2008)
Genre: Documentary, Biography, History

Divinatory Logline:
Employing rigorous patience and self-control, French tightrope walker Philippe Petit plots to perform an unauthorized acrobatic stunt by balancing at a height of 1,350 feet on a wire strung between the two towers of New York City's World Trade Center in 1974.

Inverted: Will elaborate planning and skillful maneuvers lead to success, or will the calculations prove inaccurate?

Esoteric Keys
Element: △ Fire
Astrology: ♐ Sagittarius (Philosophical, Dynamic, Experimental, Optimistic)
Numerology: XIV (Fourteen) (5)
Hebrew: ס Samekh Tent, Prop: Support, Doctrine

THE MAJOR ARCANA

XV

THE DEVIL

"This is no dream! This is really happening!
—Rosemary

The Devil as Rosemary
Film: *Rosemary's Baby* **(1968)**
Genre: Drama, Horror

Divinatory Logline:
After moving into an infamous New York apartment building, a young wife struggles with a challenging pregnancy that she comes to suspect is mysteriously connected to her actor husband's sudden career success.

Inverted: When one's ambitions trump the needs of others and principles are sacrificed, is self-destruction and spiritual downfall inevitable?

Esoteric Keys
Element: ▽ Earth
Astrology: ♑ Capricorn (Determined, Dominant, Persevering, Practical, Willful)
Numerology: XV (Fifteen) (6)
Hebrew: ע Ayin Eyes: Experience, Knowledge

XVI
THE TOWER

"It's out of control, and it's coming your way."
—Chief O'Halloran

The Tower as Fire Chief O'Halloran
Film: *The Towering Inferno* (1974)
Genre: Action, Drama, Thriller

Divinatory Logline:
At the opening of a new state-of-the-art high-rise building in San Francisco, the owner's corrupt, cost-cutting construction shortcuts result in havoc and ruin when an electrical fire breaks out that threatens the structure and traps his guests inside.

Inverted: Until the fire is extinguished, the building made safe, and courage summoned, all remain trapped in a prison of their own or another's creation.

Esoteric Keys
Element: △ Fire
Planet: ♂ Mars
Numerology: XVI (Sixteen) (7)
Hebrew: פ Pe Throat, Mouth: Speak, Word

THE MAJOR ARCANA

XVII
THE STAR

"But after a while I caught on.
I mean, I saw what they were hiring."
—Val

The Star as Val
Film: *A Chorus Line* **(1985)**
Genre: Drama, Music, Musical

Divinatory Logline:
A group of dancers narrate their life stories during a competitive cattle-call audition for a Broadway musical, baring their souls while combating despair and rejection with hope and physical effort.

Inverted: Can talent overcome doubts and obstacles when fueled by hard work and determination?

Esoteric Keys
Element: △ Air
Astrology: ♒ Aquarius (Knowledgeable, Humanitarian, Serious, Insightful, Duplicitous)
Numerology: XVII (Seventeen) (8)
Hebrew: צ Tsadi Hook: Honesty, Harvest

THE MAJOR ARCANA

XVIII

THE MOON

"Danny isn't here, Mrs. Torrance."
—Danny/Tony

The Moon as Danny/Tony
Film: *The Shining* (1980)
Genre: Drama, Horror

Divinatory Logline:
Hidden forces roam the snowbound Overlook Hotel, threatening the mental balance of a caretaker and aspiring author and jeopardizing the safety of his wife and young son, who must tap into his intuition and psychic ability to survive.

Inverted: When the veil is lifted, care must be taken and deceptions identified so that daydreams do not become nightmares.

Esoteric Keys
Element: ∇ Water
Astrology: ♓ Pisces (Fluctuating, Deep, Imaginative, Reactive, Indecisive)
Numerology: XVIII (Eighteen) (9)
Hebrew: ק Qof Back of Head: Hidden, Behind

THE MAJOR ARCANA

XIX

THE SUN

"You can bend the rules plenty once you get to the top, but not while you're trying to get there. And if you're someone like me, you can't get there without bending the rules."
—Tess McGill

The Sun as Tess McGill
Film: *Working Girl* (1988)
Genre: Comedy, Drama, Romance

Divinatory Logline:
An ambitious secretary must play by her own rules to navigate by her unscrupulous boss in order to climb the corporate ladder and achieve success in both work and love.

Inverted: When the arrogance and vanity of others casts you in shadow, what can you do to stand out?

Esoteric Keys
Element: △ Fire
Planet: ☉ Sun
Numerology: XIX (Nineteen) (1)
Hebrew: ר Resh Face: Redemption, Highest

THE MAJOR ARCANA

XX
JUDGEMENT

"Who forgives God?"
—Sharon

Judgement as Sharon
Film: *The Rapture* (1991)
Genre: Drama, Mystery

Divinatory Logline:
An aimless woman escapes from her monotonous job as a telephone operator and unfulfilling lifestyle of one-night stands by becoming a zealous born-again Christian, wife, and mother, and is ultimately driven to extremes when called upon to test her faith.

Inverted: Will her path to redemption be stalled by doubts, and will her actions harm those closest to her?

Esoteric Keys
Element: Δ Fire
Planet: ♇ Pluto
Numerology: XX (Twenty) (2)
Hebrew: ש Shin Tooth: Consume, Destroy

THE MAJOR ARCANA

XXI
THE WORLD

"I'm trying to free your mind, Neo.
But I can only show you the door.
You're the one that has to walk through it."
—Morpheus

The World as Neo
Film: *The Matrix* **(1999)**
Genre: Action, Sci-fi

Divinatory Logline:
A talented computer hacker is embroiled in a war of man versus machine when he is introduced to the hidden reality of his world and offered an opportunity to pursue liberation.

Inverted: When presented with a challenging task, will he finish the endeavor or will inertia and limited vision hold him back from success?

Esoteric Keys
Element: ▽ Earth
Planet: ♄ Saturn
Numerology: XXI (Twenty-one) (3)
Hebrew: ת Tav Sign, Cross: Covenant, Seal, Truth

THE MAJOR ARCANA

THE MINOR ARCANA COURT CARDS

THE MINOR ARCANA COURT CARDS

The Minor Arcana (or Lesser Arcana) are the 56 suit cards of the traditional 78-card tarot deck, comprising four suits of 14 cards each. Each of these suits relates to a particular aspect of our self and experience, is associated with a specific element and expression, and corresponds with a suit in a contemporary deck of playing cards.

Wands—New Activities and Ventures
Element: △ Fire
Contemporary Suit: ♣ Clubs

The suit of Wands illustrates our soul's action, movement, and growth. Encountering Wands in a reading prompts us to look at how we move through life, reach our goals, and find our purpose.

Cups—Love and Emotional Concerns
Element: ▽ Water
Contemporary Suit: ♡ Hearts

The suit of Cups relates to our emotions and matters of the heart. Cups in a reading are associated with love, feelings, and inner conflict, and they can inspire us to consider what is deeply important to us.

Swords—Intellectual Pursuits
Element: △ Air
Contemporary Suit: ♠ Spades

The suit of Swords is associated with the mind, and focuses specifically on one's decisive capabilities. Swords in a reading can indicate the need to make a decision, be it difficult or clear.

Pentacles—Business and Physical Matters
Element: ▽ Earth
Contemporary Suit: ◊ Diamonds

The suit of Pentacles denotes the material or physical world. Pentacles in a reading can speak to us about money, resources, and levels of success and prosperity.

Each of the above suits includes four court cards: Kings, Queens, Knights, and Pages. Kings and Queens represent the male and female adults, the responsible and mature aspects of the person; these are often leading characters in a reading, but can also be the person receiving the reading. Knights are generally younger men who have not yet achieved full independence or are not yet responsible for the welfare of others. Pages correspond to children, and can be either male or female.

In the CineTarot deck, I have associated the King, Queen, Knight, and Page in each suit with an iconic actor, whom I have chosen based on how their body of work and screen persona align with the meaning of the card.

KING OF WANDS

"There's a line in [The Wild One] where [my character] snarls, 'Nobody tells me what to do.' That's exactly how I've felt all my life."
—Marlon Brando

The King of Wands as Marlon Brando

Key Films:
A Streetcar Named Desire (1951)
The Wild One (1953)
On the Waterfront (1954)
The Godfather (1972)
Last Tango in Paris (1972)
Apocalypse Now (1979)

Divinatory Temperament: Driven
Marlon Brando often portrayed characters possessing the positive traits of leadership, passion, courage, and boldness as well as the negative traits of being dogmatic, forceful, domineering, and self-indulgent.

Esoteric Keys
Element: Δ Fire
Contemporary Suit: ♣ Clubs

THE MINOR ARCANA COURT

QUEEN OF WANDS

"My passions were all gathered together like fingers that made a fist. Drive is considered aggression today; I knew it then as purpose."
—Bette Davis

The Queen of Wands as Bette Davis

Key Films:
Jezebel (1938)
Dark Victory (1939)
The Little Foxes (1941)
Now, Voyager (1942)
All About Eve (1950)
What Ever Happened to Baby Jane? (1962)

Divinatory Temperament: Driven
Bette Davis often portrayed characters possessing the positive traits of being self-assured, determined, independent, and larger than life as well as the negative traits of being demanding, fickle, jealous, and temperamental.

Esoteric Keys
Element: △ Fire
Contemporary Suit: ♣ Clubs

THE MINOR ARCANA COURT

KNIGHT OF WANDS

"There's one major difference between James Bond and me. He is able to sort out problems!"
—Sean Connery

The Knight of Wands as Sean Connery

Key Films:
Goldfinger (1964)
Marnie (1964)
The Man Who Would Be King (1975)
The Untouchables (1987)
The Hunt for Red October (1990)

Divinatory Temperament: Driven
Sean Connery often portrayed characters possessing the positive traits of being sly, fearless, prideful, and impulsive as well as the negative traits of being cruel, physically abusive, and unpredictable.

Esoteric Keys
Element: Δ Fire
Contemporary Suit: ♣ Clubs

THE MINOR ARCANA COURT

PAGE OF WANDS

"Most of us have compromised with life. Those who fight for what they want will always thrill us."
—Vivien Leigh

The Page of Wands as Vivien Leigh

Key Films:
Gone with the Wind (1939)
Waterloo Bridge (1940)
That Hamilton Woman (1941)
Anna Karenina (1948)
A Streetcar Named Desire (1951)

Divinatory Temperament: Driven
Vivien Leigh often portrayed characters possessing the positive traits of being precocious, up for adventure, excited, and fearless as well as the negative traits of being impatient, proud, and prone to tantrums and breaking hearts.

Esoteric Keys
Element: △ Fire
Contemporary Suit: ♣ Clubs

THE MINOR ARCANA COURT

KING OF CUPS

"I think that making love is the best form of exercise."
—Cary Grant

The King of Cups as Cary Grant

Key Films:
Holiday (1938)
His Girl Friday (1940)
Notorious (1946)
North by Northwest (1959)
Charade (1963)

Divinatory Temperament: Emotional
Cary Grant often portrayed characters possessing the positive traits of creativity and being emotionally balanced, lighthearted, debonair, and learned as well as the negative traits of being dishonest, cold, repressed, and manipulative.

Esoteric Keys
Element: ▽ Water
Contemporary Suit: ♡ Hearts

THE MINOR ARCANA COURT

QUEEN OF CUPS

"I've only slept with men I've been married to. How many women can make that claim?"
—Elizabeth Taylor

The Queen of Cups as Elizabeth Taylor

Key Films:
A Place in the Sun (1951)
Giant (1956)
Cat on a Hot Tin Roof (1958)
Suddenly, Last Summer (1959)
Cleopatra (1963)
Who's Afraid of Virginia Woolf? (1966)

Divinatory Temperament: Emotional
Elizabeth Taylor often portrayed characters possessing the positive traits of being empathetic, sensitive, loving, and poetic as well as the negative traits of insecurity, fragility, and being overly generous and sensitive.

Esoteric Keys
Element: ∇ Water
Contemporary Suit: ♡ **Hearts**

THE MINOR ARCANA COURT

KNIGHT OF CUPS

"Only the gentle are ever really strong."
—James Dean

The Knight of Cups as James Dean

Key Films:
East of Eden (1955)
Rebel Without a Cause (1955)
Giant (1956)

Divinatory Temperament: Emotional
James Dean often portrayed characters possessing the positive traits of being idealistic, emotionally volatile, romantic, and artistic as well as the negative traits of being easily disappointed, reckless, shallow, and capable of deception.

Esoteric Keys
Element: ∇ Water
Contemporary Suit: ♡ Hearts

THE MINOR ARCANA COURT

PAGE OF CUPS

"I can live without money,
but I cannot live without love."
—Judy Garland

The Page of Cups as Judy Garland

Key Films:
The Wizard of Oz (1939)
Meet Me in St. Louis (1944)
The Clock (1945)
A Star is Born (1954)
Judgment at Nuremberg (1961)

Divinatory Temperament: Emotional
Judy Garland often portrayed characters possessing the positive traits of dreamy idealism, innocence, and deep feeling as well as the negative traits of being escapist, naive, emotionally vulnerable, and childish.

Esoteric Keys
Element: ▽ Water
Contemporary Suit: ♡ Hearts

THE MINOR ARCANA COURT

KING OF SWORDS

"It just seems silly to me that something so right and simple has to be fought for at all."
—Gregory Peck

The King of Swords as Gregory Peck

Key Films:
The Gunfighter (1950)
Roman Holiday (1953)
Moby Dick (1956)
To Kill a Mockingbird (1962)
Cape Fear (1962)
The Boys from Brazil (1978)

Divinatory Temperament: Intellectual
Gregory Peck often portrayed characters possessing the positive traits of reason, experience, and being highly analytical and principled as well as the negative traits of aloofness, cruelty, and being cold and controlling.

Esoteric Keys
Element: △ Air
Contemporary Suit: ♤ Spades

THE MINOR ARCANA COURT

QUEEN OF SWORDS

"I'm afraid of nothing except being bored."
—Greta Garbo

The Queen of Swords as Greta Garbo

Key Films:
Flesh and the Devil (1926)
Anna Christie (1930)
Grand Hotel (1932)
Queen Christina (1933)
Camille (1936)
Ninotchka (1939)

Divinatory Temperament: Intellectual
Greta Garbo often portrayed characters possessing the positive traits of intelligence, perception, independence, and being mysterious and enigmatic as well as the negative traits of deceitfulness, narrow-mindedness, pessimism, and being ill-tempered.

Esoteric Keys
Element: ⚊ Air
Contemporary Suit: ♠ Spades

THE MINOR ARCANA COURT

KNIGHT OF SWORDS

"I still find it almost impossible to relax for more than one day at a time."
—Gene Kelly

The Knight of Swords as Gene Kelly

Key Films:
On the Town (1949)
An American in Paris (1951)
Singin' in the Rain (1952)
Inherit the Wind (1960)

Divinatory Temperament: Intellectual
Gene Kelly often portrayed characters possessing the positive traits of being active, athletic, energetic, skillful, and focused as well as the negative traits of being impetuous, tactless, forceful, and controlling.

Esoteric Keys
Element: ⌂ Air
Contemporary Suit: ♤ Spades

THE MINOR ARCANA COURT

PAGE OF SWORDS

"I'm only interested in two kinds of people, those who can entertain me and those who can advance my career."
—Ingrid Bergman

The Page of Swords as Ingrid Bergman

Key Films:
Casablanca (1942)
Gaslight (1944)
Spellbound (1945)
Notorious (1946)
Autumn Sonata (1978)

Divinatory Temperament: Intellectual
Ingrid Bergman often portrayed characters possessing the positive traits of wittiness, open-mindedness, and curiosity as well as the negative traits of lack of focus, harshness, and unreliability.

Esoteric Keys
Element: ⛢ Air
Contemporary Suit: ♤ Spades

THE MINOR ARCANA COURT

KING OF COINS

"Never apologize and never explain—it's a sign of weakness."
—John Wayne

The King of Coins as John Wayne

Key Films:
Stagecoach (1939)
Red River (1948)
She Wore a Yellow Ribbon (1949)
The Searchers (1956)
The Man Who Shot Liberty Valance (1962)
True Grit (1969)

Divinatory Temperament: Physical
John Wayne often portrayed characters possessing the positive traits of being conservative, hardworking, quietly confident, reliable, and a provider as well as the negative traits of being dangerous, chauvinistic, and thriftless.

Esoteric Keys
Element: ▽ Earth
Contemporary Suit: ◊ Diamonds

THE MINOR ARCANA COURT

QUEEN OF COINS

"You only live once, but if you do it right, once is enough."
—Mae West

The Queen of Coins as Mae West

Key Films:
She Done Him Wrong (1933)
I'm No Angel (1933)
Goin' to Town (1935)
My Little Chickadee (1940)

Divinatory Temperament: Physical
Mae West often portrayed characters possessing the positive traits of being blunt, patient, practical, opulent, risqué, and savvy in business as well as the negative traits of being self-serving, a gold digger, untrusting, and insatiable.

Esoteric Keys
Element: ▽ Earth
Contemporary Suit: ◊ Diamonds

THE MINOR ARCANA COURT

KNIGHT OF COINS

"Some people seem to think that good dancers are born, but all the good dancers I have known are taught or trained."
—Fred Astaire

The Knight of Coins as Fred Astaire

Key Films:
Top Hat (1935)
Swing Time (1936)
Easter Parade (1948)
Funny Face (1957)
Silk Stockings (1957)

Divinatory Temperament: Physical
Fred Astaire often portrayed characters possessing the positive traits of being responsible, hardworking, devoted, elegant, and clever as well as the negative traits of being somewhat petty, narrow-minded, idle, and limited by dogmatic views.

Esoteric Keys
Element: ▽ Earth
Contemporary Suit: ◊ Diamonds

THE MINOR ARCANA COURT

PAGE OF COINS

"I don't stop when I'm tired. I only stop when I'm done."
—Marilyn Monroe

The Page of Coins as Marilyn Monroe

Key Films:
The Asphalt Jungle (1950)
How to Marry a Millionaire (1953)
Gentlemen Prefer Blondes (1953)
The Seven Year Itch (1955)
Some Like It Hot (1959)
The Misfits (1961)

Divinatory Temperament: Physical
Marilyn Monroe often portrayed characters possessing the positive traits of being ambitious, goal-oriented, faithful, and loyal as well as the negative traits of being erratic, immature, chronically insecure, and a procrastinator.

Esoteric Keys
Element: ▽ Earth
Contemporary Suit: ◊ Diamonds

THE MINOR ARCANA COURT

THE CINETAROT READING
LET'S GO TO THE MOVIES & MASTER THE TAROT!

THE CINETAROT READING
LET'S GO TO THE MOVIES & MASTER THE TAROT!

Three reading layouts (spreads) are provided as a starting point for you in your cinematic tarot reading.

There are a few things you will want to keep in mind that apply to each reading:

- Once the question or topic is raised, the reader shuffles the cards.
- Draw and place all the cards based on the layout (spread) you wish to use. It is up to you whether or not you let the questioner select the cards themselves or if you do it on their behalf.
- When you draw each card, think of it as a scene in a movie that is unfolding before your eyes and read them in the order drawn.
- What is the relevance of the genre, theme, and character of each card's film to the question asked?
- How do the different cards as "scenes" connect with and build upon each other?
- Is there a genre or element that appears more often than others? If so, how does this speak to the type of energy involved in the situation?

When reading the cards, always allow yourself freedom in their interpretation; consider each card's assigned meaning as a jumping-off point for further exploration. Your perception of the cards is always uniquely your own, and you should trust your innate intuition to elaborate upon the meanings of each card in a way that is expansive and flexible.

CINETAROT

THE TRAILER

I often enjoy watching the trailers for upcoming movies almost as much as the feature film itself. You can employ this simple, one-card reading using only the Major Arcana cards to answer a quick question, serve as a daily meditation, and tap into your innate intuition.

THE CINETAROT READING

THE THREE ACTS

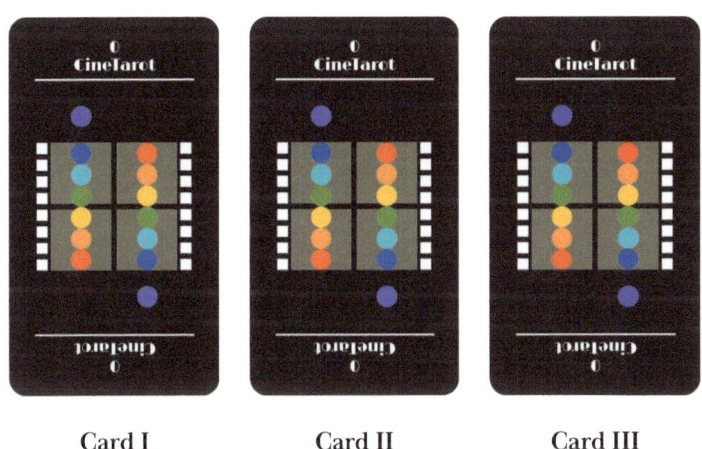

Card I   Card II   Card III

Classical filmmaking often follows a three-act structure, commonly referred to as the Setup, the Confrontation, and the Resolution. This three-part pattern aligns with some of our other key archetypal orderings of the world: time (past, present, future), the story (beginning, middle, end), and the hero's journey (departure, transformation, return). You can use this structure in your reading.

When drawing the three cards you may ask, "What is the ...

Past, Present, Future
Beginning, Middle, End
or
Setup, Confrontation, Resolution

... regarding my question/situation/concern?"

CINETAROT

THE FEATURE

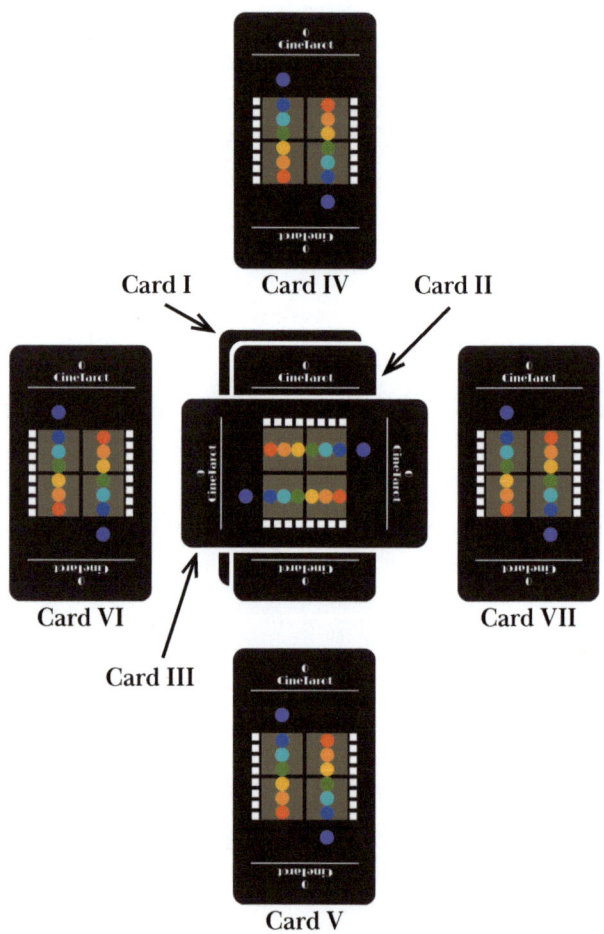

THE CINETAROT READING

The Feature layout spread elaborates on the three-act reading by using seven cards to provide greater detail.

The sequence of the card layout is as follows:

Card I: Frame of Mind
Atmosphere in which the questioner is presently working and living.

Card II: Situation
Illustrates the current concern, the immediate sphere of involvement, or obstacles which lie just ahead. This card crosses the questioner.

Card III: Swiftly Approaching
Shows what is on the horizon, usually in measures of three (e.g., three days, three weeks, three months).
Note: This card is always read upright. If upside down, invert it.

Card IV: The Distant Future/Future Soul
Shows areas that are usually spiritual in nature, which can manifest within the next one to three years.

Card V: The Foundation/The Ripening
Shows how past decisions and events have resulted in where one is today.
This card is beneath the questioner.

Card VI: The Past Six Months
Shows the sphere of influence that has come into being within the past six months.
Cross-check this with Card III.

Card VII: The Next Six Months
Shows the questioner what will transpire within the next six months and attempts to place the questioner in the proper perspective.

THE END

ABOUT THE AUTHOR

Devin Kordt-Thomas is a creative and technical professional with over 20 years of experience who works with Fortune 500 companies, local, state, and federal governments, and military and non-profit organizations. A former member of the United States Navy, he is also a skilled actor, director, writer, and producer who has performed in both the US and Europe, and is a member of the Screen Actors Guild (SAG-AFTRA) and Equity in the UK.

In addition, Devin is a certified psychic teacher, channel, and medium with the skills of clairvoyance (clear seeing), clairaudience (clear hearing), and clairsentience (clear feeling). Devin's grandmother was one of the initial extrasensory perception (ESP) test subjects who participated in academic research in the field of parapsychology at Duke University in Durham, North Carolina in the 1930s, where the first parapsychology labs were established. American by birth, in his twenties Devin was ordained as a Tibetan Buddhist monk by the former H.H. Khenpo Jigme Phuntsok and H.H. Kyabjé Drubwang Padma Norbu Rinpoche, who were recognized as two of the foremost teachers of Dzogchen. During his period of ordination, Devin had the opportunity to spend significant time cultivating an extensive daily meditation practice before returning to life as a layperson.

Devin's consultation and teaching style are hands-on and experiential. He is committed to aiding others in awakening their innate intuitive skills. His consultation practice focuses on demystifying intuition, and he works with people of all backgrounds and occupations to assist in accelerating personal growth, achieving strategic goals, navigating life events, and facilitating transformation and change.

Social Media Links:

- https://www.intuitivekey.com/
- https://twitter.com/ intuitivekey
- https://www.facebook.com/intuitivekey/
- https://www.cinetarot.com/

www.ingramcontent.com/pod-product-compliance
Lightning Source LLC
Chambersburg PA
CBHW042236090526
44589CB00006B/75